the pocket zen reader

The Pocket Zen Reader

Compiled and translated by
Thomas Cleary

SHAMBHALA
Boston & London
1999

Shambhala Publications, Inc.
Horticultural Hall
300 Massachusetts Avenue
Boston, MA 02115
http://www.shambhala.com

9 8 7 6 5 4 3 2 1

First Edition
Printed in the Canada
♻ This edition is printed on acid-free paper that
meets the American National Standards Institute
Z39.48 Standard.
Distributed in the United States by Random House, Inc.,
and in Canada by Random House of Canada Ltd.

See page 219 for Library of Congress
Cataloging-in-Publication data.

Introduction

ZEN IS TRADITIONALLY CALLED the School of the Awakened Mind, or the Gate to the Source. The premise of Zen is that our personality, culture, and beliefs are not inherent parts of our souls, but "guests" of a recondite "host," the Buddha-nature or real self hidden within us. We are not limited, in our essence or mode of being, to what we happen to believe we are, or what we happen to believe the world is, based on the accidental conditions of our birth and up-bringing.

This realization may not seem to have positive significance at first, until it is remembered how much anger, antagonism, and grief arises from the ideas of "them" and "us" based on historically conditioned factors like culture, customs, and habits of thought. Any reasonable person knows these things are not absolute, and yet the force of conditioning creates seemingly insurmountable barriers of communication.

By actively awakening a level of consciousness deeper than those occupied by conditioned habits of perception, the realization of Zen removes the strictures of absolutism and intolerance from the thinking and feeling of the individual. In doing so, Zen realization also opens the door to impartial compassion and social conscience, not in response to political opportunity, but as a spontaneous expression of intuitive and empathic capacities.

This book is a collection of quotations from the great Eastern masters of Zen. It has no beginning, middle, or end. The masters talk about the practicalities of Zen realization in many different ways, speaking as they did to different audiences in different times, but all of them are talking about waking up, seeing for yourself, and standing on your own two feet. Start anywhere; eventually you'll come full circle.

the pocket zen reader

Entry into the Way, by the Founder of Zen

There are many avenues of entry into the way, but they are essentially of just two types, referred to as principle and conduct.

Entry by principle is when you realize the source by way of the teachings and deeply believe that all living beings have the same real essential nature, but it is veiled by outside elements and false ideas and cannot manifest completely. If you abandon falsehood and return to reality, abiding stably in impassive observation, with no self and no other, regarding ordinary and holy as equal, persisting firmly, immovable, not following other persuasions, then you deeply harmonize with the principle. Having no false notions, being serene and not striving, is called entry by way of principle.

Entry by conduct refers to four practices in

which all other practices are included. What are the four? First is compensation for opposition. Second is adapting to conditions. Third is not seeking anything. Fourth is acting in accord with truth.

The practice of compensation for opposition means that when people cultivating the way are beset by suffering, they should think how in past times they themselves neglected the fundamental and pursued the trivial over countless ages, flowing in waves of existences, arousing much enmity and hatred, with no end of offense and injury. Although they may be innocent right now, they think of their suffering as the results of their own past evil deeds, not something inflicted upon them by gods or humans. Thus they accept contentedly, without enmity or complaint. Scripture says, "There is no anxiety when experiencing suffering, because of perfect knowledge." When this attitude is developed, you are in harmony with the way. Because we make progress on the way by comprehending opposition, this is called the practice of compensating for opposition.

Second is the practice of adapting to conditions. Living beings have no absolute self; they are all influenced by conditions and actions. Their experiences of pain and pleasure both come from conditions. Even if they attain excellent rewards, things like prosperity and fame, these are effects of past causes only now being realized. When the conditions wear out, they return to nothing, so what is there to rejoice about? Gain and loss come from conditions; there is no increase or decrease in the mind. When the influence of joy does not stir you, there is profound harmony with the way; therefore, this is called the practice of adapting to conditions.

Third is the practice of not seeking anything. Worldly people wander forever, becoming attached by greed here and there. This is called seeking. The wise realize that the principle of absolute truth is contrary to the mundane. Mentally at ease in nonstriving, physically they adapt to the turns of fate.

All existents are empty; there is nothing to hope for. Blessings and curses always follow each other. Living in the world is like a house on fire, all corporeal existence involves pain—who can be at peace? Because of understanding this point, we let go of all existences, stop thinking, and seek nothing. Scripture says, "Seeking is all painful; not seeking anything is bliss." Not seeking anything is clearly the conduct of the way, so it is called the practice of not seeking anything.

Fourth is the practice of acting in accord with truth. The principle of purity of essential nature is called truth. In terms of this principle, all appearances are empty; so there is no infection, no attachment, no this, no that. Scripture says, "In truth there are no beings, because it is free from the defilement of beings. In truth there is no self, because it is free from the defilement of self."

Therefore, if the wise can believe in this principle, they should act in accord with truth. The substance of truth has no stinginess: practicing charity with one's person, life, and goods, the mind has no regret. Liberated from empty personality and things, independent and unattached, with the sole purpose of getting rid of defilement, edifying people informally, this constitutes your own practice, and can also help others. It can also adorn the path of enlightenment.

As this is true of charity, it is also thus with the other five perfections, or ways of transcendence. Practicing the six ways of transcendence in order to get rid of false ideas, without objectivizing practices, is called practice in accord with truth.

Bodhidharma

Form and Shadow

Shadows arise from forms, echoes come from sounds. If we fiddle with shadows and ignore the forms, we do not recognize that the forms are the roots of the shadows. If we raise our voices to stop echoes, we are not cognizant of the fact that sounds are the roots of the echoes. To try to head for nirvana by getting rid of afflictions is like removing forms to look for shadows. To seek Buddhahood apart from living beings is like seeking echoes by silencing sounds.

So we know that illusion and enlightenment are one road. Ignorance and knowledge are not separate. We make names for what has no name. Because we go by the names, judgments of right and wrong arise. We make rationalizations for what has no reason. Because we rely on the rationalizations, argument and discussion arise. Illusion is not real:

who is right, who is wrong? The unreal is not actual: what is empty, what exists? Thus I realize that attainment gains nothing, and loss loses nothing.

Layman Hsiang

Nonduality

When the illusory body faces a mirror and its form is reflected, the reflected form is not different from the illusory body. If you only want to get rid of the reflection but leave the body, you do not realize the body is fundamentally the same as space.

The body is basically not different from the reflection. You cannot have one without the other: If you try to keep one and get rid of the other, you'll be forever estranged from the truth. Even more, if you love the holy and hate the ordinary, you'll bob in the ocean of birth and death.

Afflictions have reasons based on mind; when mindless, where can afflictions abide? If you do not bother to discriminate and grasp appearances, you will attain the way naturally in an instant. While dreaming, you act in dreams; when you awaken, dreamland doesn't exist. If you think back to waking and dreaming, they are not different from deluded dualism.

If you seek to gain by reforming illusion and grasping awakening, how is that different from involvement in commerce? When movement and stillness are both forgotten, and you are ever serene, then you spontaneously merge with reality as it is.

If you say that sentient beings are different from Buddha, then you are forever alienated from Buddha. Buddha and sentient beings are not two; this naturally comprehends all.

Pao-chih

The Nonduality of
Good and Evil

My own mind and body are blissful and happy, calm and serene, without good or evil. The body of reality is independent, without location; whatever strikes the eye is none other than true awakening.

The objects of sense are originally empty and null; ordinary people arbitrarily create attachments and fixations. Nirvana and samsara are equal; who in the world gets differential treatment? The uncontrived Great Way is natural and spontaneous; you don't need to use your mind to figure it out.

Enlightening beings are untrammeled, spiritually effective. Whatever they do is always imbued with sublime awareness. Seekers clinging to method sitting in meditation are like silkworms spitting out thread binding themselves. The essence of reality is originally completely clear; when the sickness is healed, what is the need to cling to the medicine? When you know all things are equal, you are serenely clear and open, blissfully happy.

Pao-chih

The Nonduality of Quietude and Disturbance

Seekers who disdain clamor to seek quietude are as it were throwing away flour but seeking cake. Cake is originally flour, which changes according to use.

Afflictions are not other than enlightenment. When there is no minding, there are no objects. Samsara is not different from nirvana. Craving and anger are like flames, like shadows.

The wise have no mind to seek Buddha. The ignorant cling to wrong and right. Passing all their lives in wasted toil, they do not see the sublime peak of realization of being as is. If you realize the essence of lust is empty, then even hellfire is cool.

Pao-chih

The Nonduality of Phenomena and Noumenon

The mind-monarch is independent and serene; the real nature is originally unbound. Everything without exception is Buddha-work; why should you concentrate thought in sitting meditation? Errant imaginations are originally empty and null; one need not cut off attention to objects.

The wise have no mind to be grasped; they are naturally noncontentious and peaceful. If you do not know the Great Way of noncontrivance, when can you realize the hidden mystery?

Buddhahood and ordinary life are of one kind; ordinary beings are themselves Buddhas. The common man creates arbitrary distinctions, clinging to the existence of what has none, rushing in confusion. When you

realize desire and wrath are void, what place
is not a door to reality?

Pao-chih

The Nonduality of Buddhahood and Ordinary Life

Ordinary life and Buddhahood have no distinction. Great knowledge is not different from ignorance. Why should one seek outwardly for a treasure, when the field of the body has its own bright jewel?

The right way and wrong ways are not two. When perfectly known, ordinary and sage are on the same road. Illusion and enlightenment originally have no distinction; nirvana and samsara are one suchness.

In the final analysis, clinging to objects is empty and null; only seek clear spaciousness of mind and thought. There is not a single thing that can be attained; serenely, spontaneously, you enter the ultimate.

Pao-chih

The Nonduality of Discipline and License

The actions of great people are uninhibited, not controlled by precepts and regulations. Discipline and license basically have no origin of their own, yet ignorant people are bound by them. The doings of those who know are all empty; followers get stuck on the road.

The physical eyes of enlightening beings are completely perceptive; the celestial eyes of individual illuminates have cataracts. If you arbitrarily cling to being and nonbeing in emptiness, you will not arrive at the noninterference of matter and mind.

Enlightening beings live with ordinary people; their purity is never stained by the world. Ignoramuses are greedy for nirvana; for the knowers, life and death are ultimate reality.

The nature of things is empty and has no verbal explanation; there is nothing at all in interdependent occurrence. The hundred-year-old without knowledge is a child; the child with knowledge is a hundred years old.

Pao-chih

The Nonduality of Enlightenment and Affliction

People who do not know how to practice the way therefore want to get rid of afflictions. Afflictions are originally void and null; you are trying to use the way to seek the way beyond.

The instantaneous mind is it. What is the need to seek somewhere else? The Great Way is right before the eyes; the ignorant who are deluded do not comprehend.

Buddha-nature is natural and spontaneous; it is not caused, conditioned, or fabricated. If you do not know the three poisons are unreal, you grasp at random and flounder in life, growing old. Before, when you were deluded, it wasn't too late; now you finally realize it isn't too early.

Pao-chih

Waste of Effort

Seekers cut off contusion in every state of mind, but the mind that does the cutting off is a thief. When one thief sends off another, when will you ever realize the basis of speech and silence? You may recite a thousand scrolls of scripture without understanding how the scripture applies to yourself; if you do not understand the comprehensive completeness of what the Buddha taught, you are just wasting effort following lines and counting ink marks.

Ascetic exercises and austere practices may be done seeking meritorious qualities in later life, but seeking is itself a barrier to wisdom; how could the Great Way be attained thereby? It is like crossing a river in a dream: the boatman, having crossed over the river, suddenly awakens to find he's been sleeping in bed, and has lost the way to ferry the boat.

The boatman and the people he ferries over never know each other.

Sentient beings, confused and bound up, come and go in the realms of desire, form, and abstraction, to the extremes of exhaustion. When they realize that life and death are like dreams, all their sense of seeking will spontaneously stop.

Pao-chih

Vanity

How many ignorant people in the world try to seek the Way by means of the Way! Searching widely amongst a profusion of doctrines, they cannot even save themselves. Only pursuing the confused explanations of others' writings, they claim to have arrived at the subtlety of noumenon.

Wasting a life in idle labors, they sink forever in birth and death. When polluted attachment binds the mind unrelentingly, the mind of pure knowledge afflicts itself; the forest of the cosmos of realities turns into a wasteland of brambles.

As long as you cling to yellow leaves as gold, you won't know to give up the gold for jewels. The reason you lose your mind and run around crazily is that you forcibly try to keep up appearances; you may be reciting scriptures and treatises in your mouth, but in your heart you're always lifeless.

If you realize the original mind is empty some day, the fullness of reality as is will not leave you lacking.

Pao-chih

Seek Nothing

The inner view and the outer view are both wrong; the way of Buddhas and the way of demons are both mistaken. If you are subject to these two evils, then you will reject suffering and seek pleasure. When you awaken to the root, birth and death are essentially empty; where can Buddhas or demons stay?

It is just because of the discriminations of arbitrary feelings that successive lives are isolated and alienated. The repetitious routines of mundane ways go on unceasing; if you form compulsive habits, you cannot get rid of them. The reasons for flowing in the waves of birth and death all come from arbitrary production of schemes for control.

The body is fundamentally empty and unreal; when you go back to the basis, who is calculating? Being and nonbeing can be done on your own; don't bother figuring with a confused mind. The body of sentient beings is the same as cosmic space; where can afflictions stay? Just seek nothing at all, and afflictions will naturally fall away.

Pao-chih

Principle and Practice

The Great Way is not attained by practice; talk of practice is for the ordinary and the ignorant. When you have found the principle and look back on practice, for the first time you will realize you have misused time and effort.

As long as you have not realized the great principle that permeates all, it is essential that speech and action should support each other. Do not hold to the intellectual understanding of others; turn the light of awareness back to the root, and it is not there at all.

Who understands this talk? I'll have you turn to yourself to seek. After having seen past faults and gotten rid of the sores of sensual desires, liberated, roaming free and independent, wherever I may be I sell refinement on the cheap; whoever is inspired to buy will get to be carefree just like me.

Pao-chih

The Nature of Things

The nature of things is fundamental perpetual silence, open and clear, without limits or boundaries. If you place your mind in the midst of grasping and rejecting, you will be under the influence of those two states.

If you concentrate, enter trance, and sit in meditation, focusing on an objective, setting your mind on awareness and contemplation, practicing the way like a mechanical mannequin, when will you ever arrive at the goal?

All things are fundamentally empty; there is nothing to stick to. Objects are like floating clouds, certain to disperse. When you realize the basic emptiness of fundamental essence, that will be like a fever's breaking. Don't speak of it to the ignorant, or they'll beat your body to pieces.

Pao-chih

False Buddhas

A gold Buddha can't get through a furnace, a wood Buddha can't get through a fire, and a clay Buddha can't get through water. The real Buddha sits within: enlightenment, nirvana, suchness, and Buddha-nature are all clothes sticking to the body. They are also called afflictions; don't ask and there is no vexation.

In the noumenal ground of reality, where is there to grasp? When the individual mind is not aroused, myriad things have no fault. Just sit investigating the truth for twenty or thirty years; if you don't understand, then cut off my head.

It is useless to bother to try to grasp dreams, illusions, and false appearances. If the mind does not differ, myriad things are also thus. Since it is not gotten from outside, what is there to get wrapped up in or hung up on any more? Why go on being like goats, picking up things at random and putting them in your mouth?

Chao-chou

Transcending Dualism

If you want to avoid experiencing reversal, just cut off dualism; then measurements cannot govern you. You are neither Buddha nor sentient being; you are not near or far, not high or low, not equal or even, not going or coming. Just do not cling to written letters that obstruct It, and neither side can hold you. You will escape both pain and pleasure, and escape the opposition of light and dark.

The true principle is that even reality is not really real, and even falsehood is not unreal. It is not something calculable. Like space, it cannot be cultivated. If any intellectual fabrication occurs in the mind, then it is governed by measurements. This is like divination signs—they are governed by metal, wood, water, fire, and earth. It is also like

sticky glue; the king demon can grab you,
stuck in five places, and go home freely.

Pai-chang

Provisional Teachings

If a Buddha would not speak, then people would have no hope of liberation; but if a Buddha speaks, then people pursue the words and create interpretations, so there would be little advantage and much disadvantage. That is why the Buddha said, "I would rather not explain the truth, but enter into extinction right away."

But then afterwards he thought back on all the Buddhas of the past, who had all taught the doctrines of three vehicles. After that he made temporary use of verses to explain, and provisionally established names and terms.

Originally it is not Buddha, but he told people "This is Buddha." Originally it is not enlightenment, but he told people, "This is enlightenment peace, liberation," and so on. He knew people couldn't bear a burden of ten thousand pounds, so for the time being he taught them the incomplete teaching. And he realized the spread of good ways, which was still better than evil ways.

But when the limits of good results are fulfilled, then bad consequences ensue. Once you have "Buddha," then there are "sentient beings." Once you have "nirvana," then there is "birth and death." Once you have light, then there is darkness. As long as cause and effect with attachment continue to operate, there is nothing that does not have consequences.

Pai-chang

Three Steps

The words of the teachings all have three successive steps: the elementary, the intermediate, and the final good.

At first, it is just necessary to teach people to develop a good mind. In the intermediate stage, they break through the good mind. The last stage is finally called really good.

This is what is meant by the sayings, "An enlightening being is not an enlightening being, but is called an enlightening being; the truth is not truth, yet is not other than truth." Everything is like this.

If, however, you teach only one stage, you will cause people to go to hell. If all three stages are taught at once, they'll go to hell on their own. This is not the work of a real teacher.

Pai-chang

Elementary, Intermediate, and Final Good

Realizing that the present mirroring awareness is your own Buddha is the elementary good. Not to keep dwelling in the immediate mirroring awareness is the intermediate good. Not to make an understanding of nondwelling either is the final good.

Such a person is one of the Buddhas, neither an ordinary person nor a sage. Yet do not mistakenly state that a Buddha is neither an ordinary person nor a sage. The founder of Zen said, "With no ability and no sagacity, this is enlightened sagehood." Yet if you say a Buddha is a sage, that is also wrong.

Pai-chang

Differences in Meaning

The gradations of the language of the teachings—haughty, relaxed, rising, descending—are not the same. What are called desire and aversion when one is not yet enlightened or liberated are called enlightened wisdom after enlightenment. That is why it is said, "One is not different from who one used to be; only one's course of action is different from before."

Pai-chang

Cleaning the Mind

Zen study is like washing a dirty garment. The garment is originally there; the dirt comes from outside.

Having heard it said that all sound and form, existent or not, are such filth, do not set your mind on any of it at all.

The thirty-two marks of greatness and eighty refinements of the idealized Buddha under the tree of enlightenment are all in the province of form; the twelve sections of doctrines of the canon are all in the province of sound. Right now cut off the flow of sound and form, existent or not, and your mind will be like space.

You should study in this way as attentively as you would save your head from burning. Only then will you be capable of finding a road already pre-prepared to go upon when you come to the end of your life.

If you have not accomplished that yet, if
you try to compose yourself to start learning
this when you get to the moment of death,
you will have no hope of success.

Pai-chang

Facing the End

When facing the end, generally beautiful scenes appear. According to your mental inclinations, the most impressive are experienced first. If you do not do bad things right now, then there will be no unpleasant scenes when you face death. Even if there are some unpleasant scenes, they too will change into pleasant scenes.

If you fear that you will go mad with terror at the moment of death and will fail to attain freedom, then you should first be free right now. Then you'll be all right. Right now, in respect to each and every thing, don't have any obsession at all, and do not remain fixated on intellectual interpretation. Then you will be free.

Pai-chang

Now and Forever

The cause is right now; the result is at the moment of death. When the resultant action is already manifest, how can you fear? Fear is over the past and present; since the past had a present, the present must have a past. Since there has been enlightenment in the past, there must also be enlightenment in the present. If you can attain now and forever the single moment of present awareness, and this one moment of awareness is not governed by anything at all, whether existent or nonexistent, then from the past and the present the Buddha is just human, and humans are just Buddhas.

This is, furthermore, meditation concentration. Don't use concentration to enter concentration, don't use meditation to think of meditation, don't use Buddha to search for Buddhahood. As it is said, "Reality does not seek reality, reality does not obtain reality, reality does not practice reality, reality does not see reality; it finds its way naturally." It is not attained by attainment.

That is why awakening people should thus be properly mindful, subsisting alone in the midst of things, composed, yet without knowledge of the fact of subsisting alone.

The nature of wisdom is such as it is of itself; it is not disposed by causes. It is also called the knot of essence, or the cluster of essence. It is not known by knowledge, not discerned by consciousness. It is entirely beyond mental calculation. Still and silent, essence totally realized, thought and judgment are forever ended. Just as if the flow of the ocean had stopped, waves do not rise again.

Pai-chang

The Sphere of the Enlightened

It is like the water of the ocean: even without wind there are waves everywhere. Suddenly knowing of the waves all around is the gross within the subtle; letting go of knowledge in the midst of knowing is like the subtle within the subtle. This is the sphere of the enlightened.

From this point on you really know. This is called the pinnacle of Zen, the sovereignty of Zen. It is also called knowledge of what is knowable; it produces all the various states of meditation, and anoints the heads of all spiritual princes. In all fields of form, sound, fragrance, flavor, feeling, and phenomena, you realize complete perfect enlightenment. Inside and outside are in complete communion, without any obstruction at all.

Pai-chang

Stopping and Seeing

Before the cosmic net is spread, how can its thousands of pearls be seen? When it is suddenly raised by its universal rope, the myriad eyes spontaneously open. When mind and Buddha are both observed, that is seeing; when mind and Buddha are both forgotten, that is stopping. Once concentration and insight are balanced, what mind is not Buddha, what Buddha not mind? Mind and Buddha being thus, then myriad situations, myriad conditions, are all meditation.

Ts'ao-t'ang

Tacit Accord

Nan-ch'uan was asked, "If the Great Way is not in the realm of perception or cognition, how is it realized?"

Nan-ch'uan said, "It is necessary to realize how to reach it spontaneously by tacit accord with it."

He continued, "The basis of realization does not come from perception or cognition. Perception and cognition involve objects, and only exist in relation to things. The spiritual subtlety is inconceivable; it is not relative. That is why it is said that the subtle function is mastered spontaneously, not depending on something else.

"So it is said that this is not a matter of light or dark, and is apart from being and nonbeing. It is penetrated mystically by plunging into the noumenon, unbeknownst to anyone."

The Substance of Mind

The substance of your mind is apart from annihilation and apart from eternity; its essence
is neither polluted nor pure. Calm and complete, it is equal in ordinary people and sages,
functioning responsively without convention. All realms of experience and all states
of being are only manifestations of your own
mind—do the moon reflected in water or images in a mirror have origination and extinction?

If you actually know this, you are fully
equipped. The reason that the sages have
manifested a spiritual presence to provide ex-
emplars, and have set forth a wide variety of
puzzling sayings, is simply to illustrate the
fundamental peace of the body of reality,
bringing about a return to the root.

Shih-t'ou

Beyond Mindlessness

Don't say mindlessness is itself Zen; there is an even more recondite road herein. After you have overturned the donkey-tethering stake, as you hit the south you move the north.

Huai-shan

Understanding

Questions are endless, and answers are inexhaustible: if it's a matter of curing illness, it doesn't take a donkey load of medicine.

What does that mean? When sages of yore passed on a word or half a phrase, it was something they did only because they had no other choice. If you talk a lot about different points of view, that is contrary to the essence of the way.

Indeed, the subtlety is beyond all images; the principle unifies all methods. Even while presenting many approaches, the light is hidden in the absolute.

So it seems that the way depends on the mind's awakening; it is not in words. Continuously evident, it has never been cut off. Not belaboring the mind, turn your own light around for a while. Daily activities are completely included—how can opposition stand?

Therefore it is said that the whole universe is just an illusion, unless you immediately realize the vehicle of truth and attain the mystic path all at once, forgetting all about subject and object, arriving at basic unminding, seeing through worldly troubles, understanding gangs of devils. If you effectively understand thus, it will make you happy for life. If you still don't understand, it's just because you yourselves are avoiding it.

Hui-lin

Application

Ch'eng-t'ien was asked, "How should I apply my mind twenty-four hours a day?"

He replied, "When chickens are cold, they roost in trees; when ducks are cold, they plunge into water."

The questioner said, "Then I don't need cultivated realization, and won't pursue Buddhahood or Zen mastery."

Ch'eng-t'ien responded, "You've saved half my effort."

Awakening

Once you realize universal emptiness, all objects are spontaneously penetrated: integrating the world and beyond, it contains all states of being within. If you lose the essence, there is nothing after all; if you attain the function, there is spiritual effect. The genuine path of unminding is not a religion for the immature.

Fen-yang

Body and Mind

Do you want to know what my body is? My body is the same as the whole earth.

Do you want to know what my mind is? My mind is the same as space itself.

Do you want to know what my vision is? I see there is nothing to see.

Do you want to know what I hear? I hear the unheard.

Since I have been seeing and hearing, why then do I speak of the unheard? "If you listen with your ears, after all you cannot understand; when you hear through your eyes, only then will you know."

Ssu-hsin

The Primordial Buddha

The sun rises in the east, the moon sets in the west. When one rises, one sets. From ancient times until now, people like you all know this and see this. The primordial cosmic Buddha is infinitely boundless, independent in all circumstances, in a thousand different daily affairs—why do you not see it?

It is because you still have calculation in your mind and your views are limited to effect and cause: you are not yet able to transcend religious sentiments and get beyond the shadows and traces. If you instantly understand that conditional occurrence is uncreated, you will shine with illumination like the sun and moon, envelop and support like the sky and earth.

Huang-lung Hui-nan

Subjective Feelings

When subjective feelings arrange your effort, and activity is obsessed with objects, the matter of your self is neglected; not believing in true universal knowledge in oneself, you'll never attain true awakening.

Chen-ching

Matter and Emptiness

Seeing matter itself as emptiness produces
great wisdom so one does not dwell in birth
and death; seeing emptiness as equivalent to
matter produces great compassion so one
does not dwell in nirvana.

Yun-feng

Expedients and Reality

Stop, stop! Once the Great Form had disappeared and the Pure Sound had died out, the door of expedients was opened to convey the influence of truth indirectly. With this the Three Baskets and Five Vehicles set up teachings in response to potentials. Like a nation's military forces, they were only used when unavoidable.

After that, Bodhidharma came from the West solely transmitting the mind seal. One flower blossomed in five petals, and Zen spread all over China. It was much like those born deaf becoming dumb. Why? Because you each have something that shines through all time, open as space, clear as a bright mirror: It can be experienced now, and there is certainly no possibility of it deceiving people's eyes.

But what are your eyes? Can you experi-

ence it? If you can experience it, then countless Buddhas, the Three Vehicles, the Twelve
Parts of the Teachings, the six generations of
Grand Masters, and the teachers everywhere
all shatter to smithereens in your eyes.

If you cannot experience it, ahead is
Mt. An, behind is Mt. Chu.

Yun-feng

Absolute and Relative

When the absolute is absolute, it is incomplete; within completeness there is also the relative. When the relative is relative, it is not material; even within matter, completeness remains. Deep in the night, there's the energy that brings on dawn; when the sun is at its peak, it lights up the skies.

I-ch'ing

Who's Got the Pearl?

Remain silent, and you sink into a realm of shadows; speak, and you fall into a deep pit.

Try, and you're as far away as sky from earth; give up, and you'll never attain.

Enormous waves go on and on, foaming breakers flood the skies: who's got the bright pearl that calms the oceans?

I-ch'ing

Meaningless Talk

Bottomless in depth, boundlessly vast, foaming waves flood the sky; how can you determine the current of the water? If you can discern the current of the water then you will know the source. If you don't yet know the source, for now I am speaking meaningless talk to you.

But how do you understand this "meaningless talk?" Is it that I tend to criticize people? Is this meaningless talk? Is it that speaking about worldly judgments and comparisons is meaningless talk? This is not the point.

As I see you, you are a sorry bunch. You leap up idly, and nine times out of ten crudely, merely having remembered a useless saying or an outworn speech. When you are confronted with a challenge, though, you cannot clear it up.

Nowadays there's a kind of elder who likes to instruct people by means of sayings, like giving out verbal orders in a small village. That is called slandering universal insight. It is truly hard to repent. Why don't you search your own guts? When you are lying sick and helpless on your death bed, none of the sayings you learned all your life will be of any use at all.

Ssu-hsin

Zen and the Teachings

Dharma Master Chao said, "Wisdom has the perception to find out the recondite, without any knowledge; spirit has the function of responsive understanding, without any rumination."

Even in speaking thus, the ancient certainly expended a lot of effort! How can that compare to sitting near the fireplace when it's cold, and sitting by bamboo groves and valley streams when it's hot?

Even so, I ask you, what about the ultimate matter?

Yun-feng

Eye and Cataract

Do you want to understand? The whole world is one of your eyes, the body produced by your parents is a cataract. All ordinary people ignore the indestructible, marvelously clear, unfailingly mirroring eye, and cling fast to the dust cataract produced by the relationship of their father and mother. Therefore they take illusions for realities, and grasp at reflections as the physical forms themselves.

P'u-an

Great Wisdom

Those of superior faculties and great wisdom get the point right off the bat—guidance doesn't mean gumbeating and lip-flapping. Truly awakened people with clear eyes would just laugh.

The great masters of India and China only met mind to mind—from the first there was never any "mind" to attain. But if you make a rationale of mindlessness, that is the same as having a certain mentality.

Ying-an

Spiritual Knowledge

The great enlightenment that broke down the ultimate particle manifested both substance and functions completely, expounding 5048 scrolls of teachings, each word embodying truth, pointing out 84,000 subtle ways to truth, all ending up in the ocean of essential nature. Its application is not in vain. Fact and principle are universally included, freely concentrating and expanding.

Primordially there is just a single energy, temporally expressed by means of provisional terms. It contains all things, and pervades all times. Beyond all natures and characterizations, It is a solitary light, the source of completeness, spiritual knowledge. From the eon of the void right up to now it has never perished and never been born, never increased and never decreased.

Originally there are no four kinds of birth

and six courses of being; all of them arise from false ideas. Ancient sages, out of compassion and mercy, bequeathed scriptures and established classics, wanting to get people to return to themselves. Provisionally designating the names Confucianism, Buddhism, and Taoism, they set up images to represent the heart, employed words to lead to the essential.

Thus the Confucians take Confucius and Mencius as models, Taoists study Lao-tzu and Chuang-tzu, and Buddhists search out true emptiness. The three are basically one body: that body is neither void nor material, neither existent nor nonexistent. It contains heaven and earth, including everything. It benefits sentient beings, its constant radiance shining independently.

This subtle basis is rarely expounded. The sages are long gone, and falsehood is deep; bedevilment is strong, while true teaching is weak. After Bodhidharma came from the West, not insisting on writings but just pointing to the human mind for perception of its nature and attainment of enlightenment, fortunately we had one flower blossom in five petals. When the fruit had formed, the sixth grand master disseminated it throughout the land. The mutual objective recognition of minds was called transmission of the lamp. Perfectly clear spiritual knowledge taught in accord with potentials.

There were some, however, who sunk into voidness and lingered in stillness. There were some who went frantically seeking, clinging to forms; they took up walking sticks and traveled over a thousand mountains and ten thousand rivers, not knowing for themselves that the body is the site of enlightenment. Their every thought was on objects, turning away from awakening. Retreating and forgetting halfway along the path, they sank forever into the realm of devils.

P'u-an

Transmission of Zen

Have you not read how Bodhidharma faced a wall for nine years when he first went to Shao-lin, absolutely inscrutable?

The future second grand master stood in the snow and cut off his arm, yet Bodhidharma still would not trust him.

The second grand master said, "Please pacify my mind."

Bodhidharma said, "Bring me your mind and I will pacify it for you."

The second grand master said, "Having looked for my mind, I cannot find it."

Bodhidharma said, "I have pacified your mind for you."

The mind of the second grand master opened up, and he attained great enlightenment.

When your original mind is all-pervasive, only then will you understand the meaning of Bodhidharma's coming from the West. It was transmitted successively, reaching the sixth grand master.

Teaching nowadays can hardly be compared with the wise ones of old; there is the name without the reality. Who among latter-day students knows they are turning away from awakening and getting mixed up in objects?

P'u-an

Zen Seeking

A grand master said, "With uniform equanimity, everything disappears of itself." Only then do you attain great effectiveness. When you come to the boundary of life and death, you calmly become absolutely still, without any further effort whatsoever. Just being so, like a polar mountain—does that not hit the mark?

Zen students in recent times may call themselves seekers, but wherever they take up residence they just keep false ideas in their minds, making contentious disputation a way of life. They are really pitiful.

Genuine seekers are not like this. Observe how the ancient sages since time immemorial went from community to company, got to know genuine spiritual friends, and spent ten or twenty years retreating into themselves, like dead ashes and withered trees, carefully finding out what's at the root and the stem. They had to find reality before they could adapt to conditions while remaining natural and spontaneous, worthy of the name of a Zen student or high-minded pilgrim.

If your state of mind is not clear, how can you stop arousing your mind and stirring thoughts twenty-four hours a day, like countless waves lapping all around? How can you dissolve them away?

At this point, if you have no penetrating liberation, you are just an ignorant thief stealing the community's food. When your time is up, all the mechanical knowledge and intellectualism you have acquired in your life will be of no use at all in facing death.

Even if you do countless good works all your life, you will have less and less hope of transcending birth and death. You will only get human or heavenly blessings and rewards; when the rewards are finished, as before you have no way out.

Ying-an

Lions and Geese

In olden times, Ta-sui called on over seventy
teachers. Those who had great vision were
only one or two; the rest had accurate knowledge and perception.

Hsiang-lin associated with Yun-men for
eighteen years, working as an attendant;
every word, even half a phrase, he would re-
cord on his paper robe.

By these two extremes we can see how sin-
cere the ancients were about truth. When
they reached penetration, they were empowered, transcending beyond all traps, devices,
strategies, and emotional and intellectual interpretation. This is what is meant by the
saying that the lion king does not roar at
random.

In recent times, the Zen schools are weak
and dilute. What is their problem? The prob-

lem lies in individual lack of self-trust. And where does this problem come from?

It generally comes from the basis not being correct. As long as the basis is not correct, even if you put yourself in a Zen community, you will see the Zen community as an inn; even if you talk about studying Zen and learning Zen, you will be like geese hearing thunder.

From these two extremes we can also see the difference between people of the present and people of olden times.

Ying-an

Bad Friends

Recently a kind of devil has emerged, referred to in the teachings as bad friends. They each expound different interpretations, claiming to help people.

Some teach people to stop their minds and not think at all, cutting off any stirring thought the moment it arises.

Some teach people to do nothing at all, not even burn any incense or perform any prostrations.

Some only teach people to rationally understand past and present, just like bumbling professors.

Some refer to what the ancient adepts held forth with naked hearts, and claim they were setting up schools.

Some see a student come and utter a saying that seems right, then half a day later pose a question with another saying; the student presents another saying, and if it fits they say this one has penetration.

Now tell me—do these ways of "helping people" actually live up to direct pointing to mind? Clearly there is no connection at all.

Ying-an

Dreaming and Waking

Delusion is dreaming; enlightenment is awakening. When you're deluded, you don't know it's a dream; when you wake up from the dream, then you realize it was a dream.

An ancient worthy said, "When you're in a dream, how can you know the dream is unreal? When you wake up, then you become conscious that what was in the dream doesn't exist. When you're deluded, it's like something in a dream; when you're enlightened, it's the same as waking up."

Delusion and enlightenment are originally nonexistent; it's just that the Buddhas spoke of them for remedial purposes after they had realized enlightenment.

That is why there are sayings and writings, expedient means for helping people, explaining delusion from the point of view of enlightenment, in accord with the mutual quelling of medicine and disease.

Once people are enlightened, there is fundamentally no delusion; what is the use of talking about medicine?

P'u-an

Solitary Shining

If people who study the path are intending to concentrate on Zen, they should only concentrate on the Zen of the "solitary shining of a lone lamp in the hall of nirvana." Do not set up specific periods, hoping to awaken to the path within a certain time. That is laughable.

This Zen has no trouble and no pain: the only important thing is to step back and trust completely; hang your pack high and break your staff. Stiffen your spine, and be like wood or stone inside, and like open space outside.

Suddenly the tub of lacquer comes apart, and the five clusters and eighteen elements are washed clear and clean; all beings are suddenly liberated.

Once you have seen this highway, it is not the place to stop: when you arrive at clear

understanding of universal truth, only then
will you find true and false, right and wrong,
clearly distinguished in every case. This is
called insuperably great independent spiritual mastery.

Ying-an

Steps on the Way

Those who would learn Buddhahood should just break through the seeds of karma by means of the power of great devotion, then recognize cause and effect and be wary of sin and virtue.

Detach from all mental objects, stop all thoughts: do not let either good thoughts or bad thoughts enter your thinking, do not keep either Buddhist teachings or worldly phenomena in mind.

Let go of body and mind, until you reach a state of great rest, like letting go over a cliff ten miles high, being like open space. And don't produce representations of discriminations of random thoughts arising and passing away; the moment a view sticks in your mind, use the sword of wisdom to cut it right off, not letting it continue.

Huai-t'ang

Cover the Universe

Zen is not thought, the path has no achievement; yet if not thought it is not Zen, and
without achievement it is not the path.

At this point, where do you arrive?

When you have cut through your concep-
tual faculty, how do you discriminate?

When you do not fall into consciousness,
how do you approach?

As soon as you get into the clusters and
elements, you're already a lifetime away.

What you must do is cover the whole universe, with no opinion about Buddha or doctrine, bringing it up in the midst of sharp
edges, putting it to use in heated situations.

Just trust in it thus, and naturally every
step will tread on the real ground; you can
hold still and be the master, go along with
things or spurn things, setting out and setting aside according to the time.

When you turn upward, Buddhas and devils disappear without a trace; mountains and
seas vanish.

When you turn downward, clerics are clerics, lay folk are lay folk.

You transcend seeing and hearing, get rid
of all dependence, and ride at leisure on top
of sound and form, mastering that which
startles the crowd.

Huai-t'ang

Inward and Outward Views

To cling to oneself as Buddha, oneself as Zen or the way, making that an understanding, is called clinging to the inward view.

Attainment by causes and conditions, practice and realization, is called the outward view.

Master Pao-chih said, "The inward view and the outward view are both mistaken."

Pai-chang

Objectivity
and Subjectivity

Things have never declared themselves empty, nor do they declare themselves form; and they do not declare themselves right, wrong, defiled, or pure. Nor is there a mind that binds and fetters people.

It is just because people themselves give rise to vain and arbitrary attachments that they create so many kinds of understanding, produce so many kinds of opinion, and give rise to many various likes and fears.

Just understand that things do not originate of themselves. All of them come into existence from your own single mental impulse of imagination mistakenly clinging to appearances.

If you know that mind and objects fundamentally do not contact each other, you will be set free on the spot. Everything is in a state of quiescence right where it is; this very place is the site of enlightenment.

Pai-chang

Inherent Nature

Inherent nature cannot be named. Originally it is not mundane, nor is it holy; it is neither defiled nor pure. It is not empty or existent either, and it is not good or bad.

When it is involved with impure things, it is called the two vehicles of divinity and humanity.

When mental involvement in purity and impurity is ended, the mind does not dwell in bondage or liberation; it has no mindfulness of striving or nonstriving, or of bondage or liberation.

Then, even though it is within birth and death, the mind is free; ultimately it does not commingle with all the vanities, the empty illusions, material passions, life and death, or media of sense.

Transcendent, without abode, it is not constrained by anything at all; it comes and goes through birth and death as through an open door.

Pai-chang

Realization

The basic attainment is not produced by production. Manjushri said, "It is only realized
by realization, not produced by production."
The immemorial tradition has been only to
teach people to understand the way, and not
seek anything else. If you think about it and
rationalize, that all belongs to statement and
doctrine.

All the principles of the three vehicles and
five natures I call points of practice: if you
can apply them sufficiently wherever you are,
that will do. If you discourse on the way, that
is not it; if you get obsessed, you will be im-
prisoned by that knowledge. That is also to
be called worldly knowledge. The teaching
says that those who are obsessed with canon-
ical studies are hunters and fishers, who kill
universal Buddhism for profit.

Nan-ch'uan

The Eye of the Living

Someone asked T'ou-tzu, "What is the eye of the living?"

T'ou-tzu said, "No warmth."

Superficial Imitation

A student asked T'ou-tzu, "What is avoiding superficial imitation?"

T'ou-tzu said, "I'm not fooling you."

The student asked, "What do you mean?"

T'ou-tzu said, "It won't do to teach you superficial imitation."

Subject and Object

Someone asked T'ou-tzu, "How is it when subject and object are both forgotten?"

T'ou-tzu said, "No such thing. Don't entertain such an understanding."

Bedevilment

What is bedevilment? Bedevilment means error. If you conceive intent to grasp the external, this is error. If you conceive intent to grasp the internal, this is error. If the mind is not aroused, then it is not agitated; if the mind is not agitated, this is correct.

Fu Shanhui

The Burden of Nothing

A student asked T'ou-tzu, "How about when I don't bring a single thing?"

T'ou-tzu said, "Where did you get this?"

Transformation

A single pill of alchemical elixir transmutes iron into gold; a single word of ultimate truth transforms an ordinary person into a sage. This being true even of worldly phenomena, I ask you, what is the principle behind transforming ordinary people into sages? Try to express it to everyone.

Even if you are not forthcoming, you have already said it in your gut. What is the principle behind transformation of ordinary people into sages? For now, tell me what is transformed! Don't sleep! What is it?

Is it a shout or a caning? Views like this are tantamount to the view of those who beat iron gongs on the street, telling beads and chanting.

For your part, what should you do? You must have eyes before you can discern right from wrong. Don't just go on as you are.

Time does not wait for anyone. You should make earnest effort. When you wake up after sleeping, try to see—what principle is this?

Tung-shan

The Whole Experience

High-minded mystics and pilgrims should have the eyes of Zen. When they open their mouths, they exhaust the senses of a thousand sages, make a thousand mental objects unbinding; father and mother both die, guest and host do not stand.

If you understand in this way, it is still just a little bit of Zen perceptive understanding, not the whole experience of Zen.

What is the whole experience? Go back and have some tea.

Chih-men

The Self

Chih-men was asked, "What is my self?"

He replied, "Who is asking?"

The questioner said, "Please help me more."

Chih-men said, "The robber is a coward at heart."

Zen Masters

Zen masters must clearly understand themselves, must have discriminating perception
of objective truth, and call on teachers everywhere before they can determine the religious heritage of the Zen school and see
where water and milk part ways.

Tung-shan

True Nature

The real nature of ignorance is the Buddha-nature; the ephemeral body is the body of teachings. If you can trust in this, you will inevitably save energy.

This could refer to the story of Sudhana entering the tower of Maitreya, where infinite doors of truth were everywhere; he attained universal nonresistance, and realized the nonorigination of phenomena.

This is called acceptance of phenomena as nonoriginated. Infinite realms and objects, subjective and objective, are on a hair tip without obstruction; the ten times, ancient and modern, are never apart from the immediate moment of consciousness.

But I ask you, what is the immediate moment of consciousness? The very essence of your ignorance is actually the intangible luminous nature of your fundamental awakeness.

It is because you do not realize the root source of birth and death that you cling to the false as real. Under the influence of falsehood, you fall into repetitious routines and suffer all sorts of misery.

If you can turn attention around and look back, you will realize the original true nature is unborn and imperishable, and this is why it is said that the real nature of ignorance is the Buddha-nature, and the ephemeral body is the body of teachings.

The impure elemental body has no ultimate reality at all. It is like a dream, like an illusion, like a reflection, like an echo. For infinite eons it has drifted along in the waves of birth and death, compelled by craving, never at rest for a moment, going from one state to another, piling up a mountain of bones, drinking oceans of milk.

Why? Because you have no insight and do not realize the five clusters are fundamentally empty, without any substantial reality at all; you pursue falsehood, you are subject to birth, caught up in greedy desire, unable to be free. This is why the Buddha said, "Of the causes of all miseries, greed is fundamental; if you extinguish greed, they have no basis."

If you can realize that the ephemeral body is unreal and conditional, fundamentally empty and inert, these views will not arise. There is no self, person, being, or life.

All phenomena are thus; that is why it is said that the ephemeral body is the body of teachings. When awakened, there is no thing to the body of teaching; there is only the ungraspable, mysterious universal way, listening to truth and expounding truth, the true religion with no fixations.

This is why it is said, "The essence of the root source is the natural real Buddha."

Shih-shuang

Muster Your Spirit

You should muster your spirit to penetrate the root source. Here you cannot speak of enlightenment, nirvana, thusness, liberation, transcendence, immanence, sitting in meditation, entering concentration, building bridges, or digging public wells.

Get it?

Even so, it won't do to say nothing.

When I set out on my journey, I didn't have the right intention to study Zen and learn the way; I just wanted to go to the eastern capital to listen to one or two scriptures and treatises to sustain me for everyday life.

I didn't expect that I'd wind up traveling around until I happened to meet the Zen master Shou-shan. Getting stuck by him, I simply ran with sweat.

At that time, I unconsciously bowed, but I've never gotten over my regret.

What do I regret? I regret not having dragged him off his Zen chair and given him a thrashing.

Even so, "Officially, nothing so much as even a needle is admitted; privately, even a horse and carriage can get through."

Shen-ting

Host and Guest

Ch'eng-t'ien was asked, "What is host within guest?"

He replied, "Unrecognized when met."

Then he was asked, "What is guest within host?"

Ch'eng-t'ien replied, "Poverty at home is not yet poverty; poverty on the road saddens people to death."

Finally he was asked, "What is host within host?"

Ch'eng-t'ien replied, "The words of the monarch are like strands, their dissemination is like strings."

Studying Zen

Do you want to study Zen? You must let go.

Let go of what? Let go of the four elements and five clusters, let go of consciousness conditioned over incalculable time.

Focus on right where you stand and try to figure out what the reason is.

Keep on pondering, and suddenly the flower of mind will bloom with enlightenment, illuminating the whole universe.

This can be called getting it in the mind, responding to it in action. Thereupon you can turn the earth into gold and churn the rivers into cream. Wouldn't that make life exhilarating?

Do not just memorize sayings, recite words, and discuss Zen and the way based on books. The Zen way is not in books.

Even if you can recite the teachings of the whole canon and all the masters and philosophers, they are just useless words of no avail when you are facing death.

The ancients sought illumined guides only after they themselves had awakened and understood, in order to pick out the rubble and completely purify their realization of truth.

When they could measure pounds and ounces accurately, they were like people opening variety stores carrying all sorts of goods.

Chien-ju

Avoid Drifting Off

If you really want to deal with birth and death, just avoid drifting off under any circumstances, whether you are dressing or eating, attending the calls of nature, walking, standing, sitting, or lying down.

Be like someone who sees a ferocious tiger, totally engrossed in getting away and escaping with his life.

Or be like someone on a battle front, who only wants to kill the leader of a rebellion: only when he has taken the leader's head can he rest.

Why bother with grasping and rejection, purity and defilement, profane and sacred, right and wrong, and so on?

Otherwise, it's all a waste of effort—when will peace ever be attained?

If you work in this way, it has some relevance to birth and death; otherwise, it's all contrivance, without benefit on the way. A former teacher said, "Don't get stuck in small successes, you must reach the state of the ancients before you attain freedom in life and death." Otherwise it is all something on the shore of birth and death; there's really no end in sight.

Chien-ju

The Experience
of Zen Study

The experience of studying Zen is like hiding your body in fire: even if you have iron guts and a brass heart, here they will surely melt and flux.

Even so, space must shatter to smithereens and earth sink away before you will have a way to turn around. Only at such a time should you get a thrashing.

Chien-ju

Other Things

Studying Zen, learning the way, is originally for the sake of birth and death, no other thing.

What do I mean by other things? Arousing the mind and stirring thoughts right now; having contrivance and artificiality; having grasping and rejecting; having practice and realization; having purity and defilement; having sacred and profane; having Buddhas and sentient beings; writing verses and songs, composing poems and odes; discoursing on Zen and the way; discoursing on right and wrong; discoursing on past and present.

These various activities are not relevant to the issue of birth and death; they are all "other things."

Chien-ju

Virtue and Enlightenment

Cultivating blessings without cultivating the way has been scorned by Zen masters as delusive; practicing charity with the wrong attitude is pointed out in scripture as demonic activity.

From this point of view, the foremost blessing is not comparable to the teaching of the mind ground. If you do not know the mind, it will certainly be hard to eliminate the seeds of greed, wrath, and folly: even if you have heavenly blessings, after having risen you will sink again, like a bird with its feet tethered flying up in vain.

Therefore cultivating blessings is not as good for students of the way as is seeing essential nature. If you can see essential nature, then blessings are no longer limited.

Ta-tu

The Quest

The quest of real followers of the path is just to oppose birth and death; they do not look for it in the sayings found in various sources in ancient and modern books. They just step back into themselves and bring it to mind, coolly yet keenly, at the very root and stem.

Suddenly their hands slip, they lose their footing, and they're lost: this is graduation from the study of a lifetime. Perceiving independently, like a solitary lamp, for the first time they are manifestly empowered.

They are like mountains; how could the fears of life and death shake them any more?

Ying-an

Unminding

If you want to understand readily, just be un-minding at all times and all places, and you will naturally harmonize with the path.

Once you are in harmony with the path, then inside, outside, and in between are ultimately ungraspable; immediately empty yet solid, you are far beyond dependency.

This is what ancient worthies called "each state of mind not touching on things, each step not positioned anywhere."

Ying-an

The Key to
Spiritual Effect

The reason the ancients had spiritual effect in learning the way was that the thieving mind had died completely. If the thieving mind does not die entirely away, there is no way you will ever attain self-fulfillment.

Speaking in simple terms, if you kill off a tenth of the thieving mind, you've learned a tenth of the way; if you kill off five tenths of the thieving mind, you've learned five tenths of the way. When the thieving mind is entirely gone, everything is the way.

Ming-pen

Swifter and Slower Ways

Worldly afflictions are as extensive as an ocean, noisy and clamorous; but they all arise from the thoughts in your own mind. When not a single thought is conceived, you are liberated from them all.

Since it depends on one's own self, how hard could it be? Attaining Buddhahood shouldn't take even a finger snap.

Viewed in this way, it seems very easy; but even so, you must be the one to do it. An ancient also said, "The moment you produce a thought, it is an object; just don't have a single thought, and objects disappear, so mind dies out spontaneously, and there is nothing more to pursue."

Those who already have good roots will understand this kind of talk the moment they hear it. Those who may be slower should look into it over and over—ultimately what principle is this?

Ta-tu

Know Your Own Mind

You really have to know your own fundamental mind before you can stop and rest.

If you know your mind and arrive at the fundamental, that is like space merging with space.

Ta-tu

Emptiness

Bodhisattvas in the beginning stage first realize that all is empty. After that, they realize
that all is not empty.

This is nondiscriminatory wisdom. It is
what is meant by the saying that "form itself
is emptiness."

It is not emptiness as annihilation of form;
the very essence of form is empty.

The practice of bodhisattvas has emptiness as its realization. When beginners see
emptiness, this is seeing emptiness; it is not
real emptiness. Those who cultivate the way
and attain real emptiness do not see emptiness or nonemptiness; they have no views.

Tao-hsin

Objective Reality

If objective reality is not manifest, what awakening at all is there to talk about? It is all escapism and reality-avoidance. What do you call this? It is like putting a stone on grass; when you remove the stone, habit energies are still there as before.

You must understand wherever you are; you must be master of the objective world, avoiding compulsion by sense objects. It is very, very difficult; there are a thousand difficulties, a myriad difficulties.

Ta-sui

Practice

Just detach from all sound and form, but do not dwell in detachment, and do not dwell in intellectual interpretation—this is practice.

As for reading scriptures and studying the doctrines, according to worldly conventions it is a good thing, but from the perspective of one who is aware of inner truth, it chokes people. Even those in the tenth stage cannot escape completely; they flow into the river of birth and death.

Pai-chang

Along the Way

Ta-sui was asked, "What is the point to concentrate on along the way?"

He replied, "Don't be self-conceited."

Immaturity

As soon as you get some sense of contact, you want to be teachers of others. This is a big mistake.

Ta-sui

The First Point

Ta-sui was asked, "What is the very first point?"

He replied, "Don't think falsely."

Sincerity

The worthies of past ages all sought the truth and did not deceive themselves. They were not like moths throwing themselves into flames, destroying themselves in the process.

Ta-sui

Everywhere

Ta-sui was asked, "Buddha's truth is everywhere; so where do you teach students to
plant their feet?"

He replied, "The vast ocean lets fish leap
freely; the endless sky lets birds fly freely."

Foresight and Diagnosis

You must discern the result in the cause, and
discern the cause in the result.

Ta-sui

What and Who

A student asked T'ou-tzu, "What is 'turning the wheel of the teaching in fire'?"

T'ou-tzu said, "Understood everywhere."

The student asked, "What about after understanding?"

T'ou-tzu said, "No wheel of teaching to turn."

The student asked, "What should be done about temporary lapses in presence?"

T'ou-tzu said, "Who informs you about them?"

No Mistake

Someone asked T'ou-tzu, "How is it when there is no mistake moment to moment?"

T'ou-tzu said, "Bragging."

The Obstruction of Nonobstruction

A student asked T'ou-tzu, "What is the one expression of Nonobstruction?"

T'ou-tzu said, " 'Thus.' "

The student said, "This is still an obstruction."

T'ou-tzu said, "Yes, it is."

Mind and Matter

Resistance does not mean walls and fences, nonresistance does not mean open space. If you can understand in this way, mind and matter are fundamentally the same.

Tsu-hsin

The Eye

In the teachings it says that all compounded things are like dreams, illusions, bubbles, and shadows; they are like dew and like lightning, and should be seen in this way.

What eye do you see with? When you have fully attained this eye, you will see the mountains, rivers, and earth do not ruin or adulterate yourselves, nor do yourselves ruin or adulterate the mountains, rivers, and earth. There is no more sacred doctrine therein to make for understanding or obstruction. And there is no ordinary convention to make for understanding or obstruction.

But can you believe it? If you can believe it, then consciousness conditioned by ignorance turns into endless meditation. If you can't believe, endless meditation turns into consciousness conditioned by ignorance.

Tsu-hsin

Independence

To know by thinking is secondary; to know without thinking is tertiary. It is essential for the individual to directly bear responsibility and put down the two extremes of clarity and unclarity from your learning hitherto; when you reach the state of cleanness and nakedness, then you must go on over to the Beyond, where you kill Buddhas when you see Buddhas, kill Zen masters when you see Zen masters.

In Zen, this is still the work of servants. Independent people should not seek Zen or Tao or mystery or marvel from the mouths of old monks sitting on the corners of meditation seats and stuff that into stinking skinbags, considering it the ultimate principle. Isn't this a mistake?

Ying-an

Understanding Zen

In reading scriptures and studying the doctrines, you should turn all words right around and apply them to yourself.

All the verbal teachings point to the inherent nature of the immediate mirroring awareness. As long as this is not affected by anything, existent or otherwise, it is your guide. It can shine through all realms, whether they exist or not.

This is adamantine wisdom, wherein you have your share of freedom and independence. If you cannot understand in this way, then even if you could recite the whole canon and all its branches of knowledge, that would only make you conceited. Paradoxically, it shows contempt for Buddha; it is not true practice.

Pai-chang

False Teachers

Even if you seek tranquillity, delight in goodness, and search for the source, if you don't meet someone with genuine true knowledge and understanding, it will turn instead into major error. The fault lies in false teachers.

P'u-an

Cleaning House

If you want to cut off the path of birth and death, you should throw away everything you have always treasured in your mind. Then your six senses will naturally be clean and naked. One day you will have a flash of insight and no longer worry that the road of birth and death will not be cut off.

If you do not make real application basic, and instead desire lots of knowledge and intellectual understanding, considering this the subtlety of self-realization, then you will be blown by the wind of knowledge and intellectual understanding, making you colder and hotter, constantly occurring to you, so that your nose is stuffed up and your head is unclear, day in and day out. This is a calamity you bring on yourself—it is not the fault of another.

Ying-an

Verbal Teachings

The verbal teachings of Buddhas and Zen masters that have come down from the past are like bits of tile used to knock on a door; it is a matter of expediency that we use them as entrances into truth.

For some years now, students have not been getting to the root of the aim of Zen, instead taking the verbal teachings of Buddhas and Zen masters to be the ultimate rule. That is like ignoring a hundred thousand pure clear oceans and only focusing attention on a single bubble.

Ying-an

The Way of Buddhas and Zen Masters

The way of Buddhas and Zen masters is open as cosmic space, vast as the ocean—how can careless mediocrities tell of it? And how can it be measured like feet and inches, or calculated like thatch?

Only those of great faculties, great capacity, and great power, exerting great intensity, stomp right through where not a single thought has arisen, not a single bubble has emerged, after that sitting and reclining on the heads of the Buddhas and Zen masters. Only then do they have a little bit of realization.

Hsueh-yen

Act on Reality

In learning this path, it is only important to walk on the real ground, to act on the basis of reality. The slightest phoniness, and you fall into the realm of demons.

If your vision is perfectly clear and you are not confused by objects twenty-four hours a day, then you gain power. If your vision does not penetrate freely, how can you do what is beyond measure?

An ancient said, "Even if there is anything beyond nirvana, I say it too is like a dream illusion." If your own eyes are not yet open, how can you understand?

The conduct of those transcendent people is like diamond flames, like a raging fire—there is no way for you to get near. It is not forcibly contrived; it is so by nature.

Liao-an

Acquiescence

Every point you find impenetrable in the realm of work on the way is just your own mind making obstacles. If this mind would acquiesce completely, you would arrive at the stage of Buddhas and Zen masters immediately, and there would be nothing supposedly obstructing you any more.

The right attitude for studying the way is just complete spontaneous acquiescence. Who cares whether it takes twenty or thirty years—you'll be naturally at peace, without the slightest bit of doubt or confusion. How can there be any obstruction again after spontaneous acquiescence? How can anyone arrive by way of externals?

Ming-pen

One Source, Same Aim

Ultimately, why should people who brush aside the weeds looking for the *way* necessarily be concerned with the cycle of birth and death? It is essential to clarify the one actuality that is prior to "sentient beings" and "Buddhas."

If you try to look for it in quietude, it goes and crouches in clamor; if you look for it in clamor, then it stands in quietude. If you want to place it in the realm of nothingness, yet it is a living thing.

How can you get it? If you let action and stillness flow from one source, and apply the ancient and the modern to the same aim, polishing and refining over and over, without getting hung up over the time it may take, then naturally the autumn water will become still, and the golden waves will suddenly appear, shining through the mountains, rivers, and earth, the myriad distinctions and thousands of differences.

It is only because temperaments are not the same that there are differences in quickness and slowness.

Chueh-an

Two Ailments

In learning the way there are not more than two kinds of sickness: either lingering in clear stillness, or staying in the midst of confusion and disturbance. Those who are fierce and intense will sharply reject both of these and leap through and beyond the Other Side in one bound: not only do other and self, sound and form, subject and object all vanish at once; no sign of birth and death can be found at all.

Only then can you be called an uncontrived free wayfarer with nothing more to learn, having attained the great cessation, great rest, and great bliss. But when you get to such a state, you can only be said to have realized yourself and understood yourself; if you talk about the thirty-six rivers of Shu, there are yet great difficulties ahead.

Wu-chun

Complete Potential

Complete potential responds universally; perception is before activation of potential. Leaving aside perception for the moment, what about the aftermath of response?

If you do not make your steps broad and pay close attention, you will fall into stagnant water, with no hope of getting out.

If you can turn around and look at your shadow, this is already being slow about it.

When I talk like this, does it seem like my tongue is dragging on the ground? This is why in the *Lankavatara-sutra* Buddha says that mind is the source and emptiness is the door to the truth.

All the different speech of the world, mundane and transmundane, is an immense state of liberation.

Is this not what Buddha said, that only mind is the source? Where do you still worry you will not penetrate? What place is not your self?

If, however, you get the gist immediately in this way, I already know you will have understood it dogmatically. Let those with the adamantine eye discern!

Huai-t'ang

Everywhere

Everywhere is where followers of the way lay down their lives. Everywhere is where followers of the way tune their minds.

Everywhere is the treasury of endless capacities of followers of the way. Everywhere is not everywhere; it is called everywhere.

I often see students who are narrow-minded, who gain a little bit in a limited context, with a limited perspective, and consider this enough, immediately insisting on stopping and resting. Eating their fill and sleeping, not taking care of anything at all, they consider themselves lively, but they are destitute ghosts.

Hui-k'ung

Awareness

When aware that the content of awareness is empty, empty awareness is complete. When hearing the content of hearing is finite, finite hearing does not remain.

Even if you can see in this way, you are already involved in process. Has it not been said, "If feelings retain notions of the holy, this is still involvement in external objects; if the idea of self is not forgotten, it's the same as leaking."

How could it be possible to suppose that discoursing on mind and nature and lecturing on Zen and the path are effective vehicles to the source?

Wu-chien

Progressive Realization

Each form, each particle, is a Buddha. One form is all Buddhas. All forms, all particles, are all Buddhas. All forms, sounds, scents, feelings, and phenomena are also like this, each filling all fields.

This is the gross within the subtle; this is a good realm. This is the cognition and perception of all those in progress; this is the exit in life and entrance in death of all those in progress, crossing over everything, existent and nonexistent.

This is what is spoken of by those in progress. This is the nirvana of those in progress. This is the unexcelled Way. This is the spell that is peer to the peerless. This is the foremost teaching, considered the most profound of all teachings. No human being can reach it, but all enlightened ones keep it in mind, like pure waves able to express the purity and pollution of all waters, their deep flow and expansive function.

All enlightened ones keep this in mind. If you can be like this all the time, no matter what you are doing, then the body of pure clear light will be revealed to you.

Pai-chang

Detailed Instructions

If we are to discuss the conditions of this great matter, although it is originally inherent in everyone, actually complete in each individual, lacking nothing at all, nevertheless for beginningless ages the seeds of the root of attachment, subjective ideas, and emotional thinking have become so deeply ingrained as habits that they block and cover the subtle light and thwart its real true function. Living totally within the shadows of subjective ideas of body, mind, and the world, you therefore flow in the waves of birth and death.

When Buddhas and Zen masters appear in the world, everything they say, all their various techniques, expounding Zen and the teachings, are without exception tools for breaking attachments according to the situation; basically there is no real doctrine to give people. So-called cultivation is just clearing away the reflections of force of habit and false thinking, according to ones own mind; insofar as effort is applied to this, it is called cultivation.

If false thinking suddenly stops for an instant, and you see through your own mind, the vastness of its original perfect light, the purity of its original state, no thing in it at all, this is called awakening. There is nothing to be awakened or cultivated other than this mind.

Because the substance of mind is like a mirror, the reflections of subjective thinking climbing around on objects are just dust and dirt on the true mind. That is why it is said, "The forms of thoughts are dust, the feelings of consciousness are dirt." If false thoughts are melted down, the original substance itself appears: it is just like polishing a mirror—when the dirt is cleaned off, clarity appears.

It is naturally like this, but we humans have accumulated eons of ingrained habits that have become hard and fast; the roots of self-love are deep and hard to pull out.

In the present life, if we have the fortune to know for ourselves what is intrinsic through the inner influence of inherent insight outwardly inspired by good friends, so we aspire to understand and shed birth and death, to tear out the very root of immeasurable ages of birth and death all at once, how could this be a small matter?

If you are not a person of great power and capacity who can bear it alone and plunge right in with a single sword, it is truly the most difficult thing there is. When an ancient said that it is like opposing ten thousand people all alone, he wasn't fooling!

On the whole, in this final age of the teaching, there are many practitioners, but few who succeed in genuine appreciation and application; there are many who waste power and few who attain power. Why is this? Generally because they have not taken a direct approach; they just use their subjective feelings to evaluate things based on previously learned opinions, intellectual interpretations, and verbal expressions. Suppressing random thoughts, they work at the gateway of shadows of a light. First they take mysterious words and marvelous sayings of ancient people and store them in their chests, making them out to be real doctrines, taking them for their own knowledge and vision, not knowing that it is utterly useless in this context.

That is precisely what is meant by the saying, "Reliance on others for understanding blocks the gateway of one's own awakening."

Now if you are going to do the work, first you must set aside intellectual interpretations and just work precisely on one thought, certain faith in the original purity of your own mind. Completely untrammeled, round and bright, it fills the universe. Originally there is no body, mind, or world, and no false ideas or emotional thinking. This one thought, itself originally unconceived, manifests all sorts of objects, all illusory, unreal— they are only reflections appearing in the true mind.

When you see through them in this way,

then in the emergence and disappearance of wandering thoughts you can see for sure at a glance where thoughts arise and where they pass away. Focus your effort in this way, and no matter what wandering thought may occur, the moment you confront them they shatter, melt, and crumble away. Do not go along with them, and don't continue them. This is what Yung-chia meant when he said "It is essential to cut off the continuing mind."

After all, the insubstantial drifting mind is fundamentally rootless; under no circumstances should you make it out to be something real lying in your chest. The moment it appears, repudiate it; once you repudiate it, then it vanishes. Don't try to suppress it, for you will go along with it, making it like a gourd bobbing on water.

You just need to set body, mind, and the world to one side, and bring up this one thought, simply and precisely, like a precious sword across the sky—whether Buddha or devil, you cut them off equally, like cutting through tangled threads, pushing them to the side to move ahead—so-called direct, straightforward mindfulness of reality as such. Straightforward mindfulness involves no thought; if you can observe without thought, you can be said to be heading for the wisdom of Buddhas.

The very first inspiration to practice requires certain faith in the teaching of mind alone. Buddha said the triple world is only mind, myriad things are only consciousness. So many Buddhist teachings only explain this saying, clearly enabling every individual to believe in it. The two main roads of the ordinary mortal and the sage are simply the two routes of confusion and awakening within one's own mind. All good and bad causes and effects are totally ungraspable outside this mind.

Our subtle essence is natural; originally it is not in the domain of realization, so how can it get lost? Now when we say it is lost, that just means one does not understand there is originally not a single thing in one's own mind, and one has not realized the original emptiness of body, mind, and world; being obstructed by them, it is said to be lost. Operating only with the fluctuating mind thinking subjectively, taking that for truth, people therefore take all sorts of illusions associated with objects of the six senses to be realities.

Now when you aspire to go against the current and attain transcendence, it is totally essential to shed your previous knowledge and understanding completely. No knowledge or technique is applicable—it is just a matter of seeing right through your own present body, mind, and world: all are illusory reflections of ephemeral light manifested in your own mind, like images in a mirror, like the moon reflected in water.

Look upon all sounds as like wind passing through the trees; look upon all objects as like clouds floating through the sky, all of them illusory, unreal things. Not only are externals like this: your own mind's subjective notions and emotional thinking, the seeds of the roots of all attachments, forces of habit, and psychological afflictions, are empty, ephemeral, illusory, unreal.

Looking deeply in this way, whenever a thought arises be sure to check where it's going. Don't let it go too easily, and don't be deceived or deluded by it. When you work in this way, you are approaching true attentiveness. Other than this, if you spread out mysteries and marvels, knowledge and views, techniques and methods to linger over, you are completely out of touch.

So the fact is that explaining how to do the work is also just an expedient. It is like the use of military force: weapons, being instruments of ill omen, are only to be used when it cannot be avoided. Similarly, when the ancients spoke of bringing up sayings to study Zen, it was all because they could not help but do so.

Although there are many kung-an, the saying "Find out who is really invoking the name of Buddha" is the one with which it is most easy to attain power in the midst of worldly toils. While it is easy to attain power with it, nevertheless it is like a piece of tile used to knock on a door; in the end it is to be discarded, though not without putting it to use once.

To employ this to do work right now, you must trust it completely, rely on it steadily, and persevere in it continuously. Be sure not to vacillate; it won't do to be like this today and like that tomorrow, worrying you won't get enlightened, or disliking this as not mysterious or marvelous—these thoughts and calculations are all obstructions. It is necessary to explain them away first, so doubts and worries do not arise on specific occasions.

When you have done the work to the point where you have attained some power, and external objects do not enter in, but there are afflictions inside the mind arising arbitrarily in unruly ways—it may be desirous thoughts coming out, or psychological turmoil, or hang-ups of all sorts, tiring your mind and sapping your energy, beyond your control—these are seeds of forces of habit, stored in your repository consciousness over incalculable ages, now coming out under the pressure of the work.

It is absolutely necessary that this point be distinctly clear. You must see through these phenomena to begin with and pass right through them. Be sure not to be trapped by them, be sure not to fiddle around with them, and be sure not to take them for realities. Just clarify your spirit, exert yourself, and pluck up your courage: take up the saying you are looking into, and use it to chase away these thoughts when they arise. There are originally no such things in us—ask where they come from, and ultimately what they are; be sure to see what they come down to.

Keep on pushing like this, and you'll simply make spirits and ghosts weep; you'll obliterate tracks and traces. Strive to drive them all into extinction, not leaving any at all. Apply effort in this way, and you'll naturally see some good news. The moment you push all the way through, all errant thoughts will fall away at once, like the shadows of flowers in the sky dropping, like the waves of a mirage settling.

Once you've gone through this, you'll gain immeasurable ease and comfort, immeasurable freedom. This is the beginner's empowerment; it is not considered a mysterious marvel.

Now when you reach ease and freedom, still do not become joyful. If you become joyful, the demon of joy will stick to your mind and add yet another kind of obstacle.

If you come to forces of habit and seeds of the root of attachment that are so firmly rooted deep in the unconscious that a saying can exert no effect on them, then look into where the mind's perception cannot reach.

If you can't do anything yourself, then perform prostrations before Buddhas, recite scriptures, and practice repentance. You also need to inwardly hold the essence of sacred spells, relying on the esoteric symbols of Buddha to dispel these obstacles. Because the esoteric spells are all impressions of the indestructible mind of Buddhas, when we use them it is like wielding a diamond club, smashing everything into atomic particles. The secret of the mind seal of the Buddhas and Zen masters since high antiquity is not beyond this. Therefore it is said that the Buddhas of the ten directions hold the essence of spells, attaining unexcelled universal true enlightenment.

In the schools of the Zen masters, it was feared that this would fall into common emotion, so it was kept secret and not spoken of; it's not that it wasn't used. This should be done on a regular daily basis; over a long period of time it becomes pure and mature, and very much power is gained. Just refrain from wanting or seeking spiritual experiences.

Han-shan

Direct Realization

The matter of Zen is only realized directly by people of superior faculties; those of mediocre and lesser potential have no part in it. Without opening any doors or setting out any pathways, it presents the whole right to your face, to be personally realized and personally attained, without any further how or why.

Speaking in extreme terms, the statement, "This very mind is Buddha" says it all. This statement, however, is still in the realm of inducement. If you actually understand it, every breath is cut off, all conceptions are cut off—you just silently accord, that's all. Otherwise, you are mistaking your consciousness for the master.

Ta-tu

The Poison Sea

If Zen students have not shed their stage of vision and have not forgotten their knowledge of principle, they fall into the poison sea of liberation. Their emotionalized perception is not yet erased, their objectivized perceptions are not empty: they are totally a mass of ignorance, composed of conditioned consciousness.

As long as the mass of ignorance composed of conditioned consciousness is not broken up, and the poison sea of liberation is not dried up, this is precisely the root of birth and death.

Ch'ih-chueh

Universal Good

Buddha said to the bodhisattva Universal Eye, "Is there anyone who can tell the whereabouts of the various illusory appearances in magical writings?" He answered, "No."

Buddha said to Universal Eye, "Since even the illusory appearances in illusions cannot be explained, how about the esoteric physical realm of the Universally Good bodhisattva, the esoteric verbal realm of the Universally Good bodhisattva, the esoteric mental realm of the Universally Good bodhisattva? Yet if you enter into them, you can penetrate and can see."

It is bright in the mind's eye, radiant in material form; don't call the silver world a temporary silver citadel.

Pei-chien

No Separation

One moon appears everywhere in all bodies of water; the moons in all bodies of water are contained in one moon. This is a metaphor for one mind producing myriad things and myriad things producing one mind. This refers to dream illusions, flowers in the sky, half-seeming, half empty.

What if drifting clouds cover the sky; where is the clear light in the waters? Here, if you open up the eye of true insight, you will see that the moon has never not been there, the light has never disappeared—light and dark are as one, death and life have no separation.

Hsueh-yen

No

When you look into the word "No," it is only essential to arouse a feeling of doubt about the word "no" and look into it. Ask yourself, why did Chao-chou say the word "No"? Look into it this way twenty-four hours a day.

When you are looking into it, don't ask whether there is thinking going on or not; thinking and not thinking are both in the realm of illusion.

At present it is only necessary for you to keep up the feeling of doubt at the saying you're looking into. You do not need to think about anything at all; any thought you conceive apart from the saying you're looking into, no matter whether it is a thought of Buddha or a thought of the teaching, is not right mindfulness, but a seed of birth and death.

People who are really and truly doing the

work are intent on it twenty-four hours a day, as intent as if they were saving their heads from burning, as if they were facing ten thousand adversaries single-handed. When would they find the leisure time to be obsessed with their personal lives or worldly conditions? And what leisure do they have to seek edification from others? What idle time, furthermore, do they have to question others, to look for sayings and statements, to seek interpretation and understanding?

Some people are at a loss and helpless if they don't get instruction from someone for three days. They are all in a whirl, chasing illusions; they are not doing the work.

In general terms, people doing the work are like thieves intent on stealing others' valuables. When they are walking, they are walking intent on stealing; and when they are sitting they are sitting intent on stealing. When at leisure they are intent on stealing at leisure, and when in a hurry they are intent on stealing in a hurry. Why would they willingly reveal their intention of stealing, so others could see? The keener their intent to steal, the more they keep it a hidden secret. If you can be like this in every state of mind, in every moment of thought, and continue thus unremittingly for a long time, surely you will reach the stage of the ancients.

This is not like those who are unable to be the master steadily twenty-four hours a day, but just want to forcibly be the master while going along with the whirl of random thoughts, rushing to their cushions to imitate a posture while frantically seeking, thought after thought, unwilling to stop and rest. How can they ever find accord?

Ming-pen

Sameness and Difference

In the Zen school there is a type of brilliant people who start out by attaining a semblance of understanding at teachers' words, then take it at that. At that time, if the teachers have no leisure to question whether they are enlightened or not enlightened, they let them go for the while.

At this point they teach their own insight to others; now they don't want anyone to doubt sayings, they only value ready-made understanding. Thus they drag each other down into a web of intellectual views. When they talk it seems like Zen, but their actions are totally unconnected.

There is a kind of beginner who is ignorant and slow, who hears that to study Zen one should look into a saying and arouse a great feeling of doubt, after which one may suddenly awaken insight, and then spends twenty or thirty years firmly relying on a saying for contemplation, continuously from beginning and end, unwilling to let it go. Eventually illusions suddenly vanish completely and they awaken.

After that, whenever learners ask them for help, they invariably want to have people look into sayings, arouse a feeling of doubt, and make concentrated effort. With teachers like this, while it is hard to make progress to insight, nevertheless they do not wind up ruining people's natures.

Ever since there have been Zen schools, although they speak of simply pointing to the human mind, they have employed countless different methods. Relying on the one principle of simple pointing, the teachers have guided differently in accord with people's dispositions as well as their own personal experience of enlightenment; yet in every case the supreme principle and the ultimate end were the same, the great matter of understanding and shedding birth and death, nothing else.

People's mentalities have many differences, and they cannot just "crap once and be done." There are statements to the effect that one should also see others after awakening, and there are statements to the effect that one still needs practice after attaining insight: these are for cases where awakening has not been thorough, and people still have different attachments and cannot remove sticking points and untie bonds for others.

Thus there are recommendations to see others or practice more, but for those who are enlightened once and for all there are no such teachings.

Although the ancients did not look into model stories and arouse the feeling of doubt, it must be remembered that their attitude before enlightenment was thoroughly dissimilar from that of people today. If you taught people today not to make concentrated effort, every one of them would sit inside a web of delusions.

An ancient said, "Relying on others to formulate understanding blocks the door of your own awakening." The *Scripture of Complete Enlightenment* says, "If people in the degenerate age want to attain the way, don't make them seek enlightenment, for they will only increase their formal learning, which will inflate their idea of themselves."

Ming-pen

Buddha's Treasury of Light

I observe the Buddha's treasury of light producing all oceans of lights: whether sage or ordinary mortal, animate or inanimate being, none are not endowed with this body of light and openly demonstrating the function of this light. Root and branches are completely included, withdrawal and expansiveness are uninhibited, self-help and helping others are inexhaustible.

It is like the sun rising in the sky, shining on all without discrimination. The illuminator and the illumined are both empty and silent, while all sentient beings benefit from the light, accomplishing their individual tasks. They never know each other, and don't rely on each other: no one knows why it is as it is, but that does not diminish the illumination provided by the sunshine. This is like the inherent spiritual light; it is not gotten from another, yet those who are blind to it do not awaken.

Are they blind to the end? If they can return to the light in an instant, it will be the same as having been there all along. So it is said, "The path is not far from people; it is realized in this very mind." Is that not so?

Liao-an

The Pure Land

The Pure Land is only mind; there is no land outside of mind. In this land that is only mind, there is no east in the east, no west in the west—all directions are contained in it.

The so-called Buddha-lands numerous as atoms in the ten directions are all realms within one's own Pure Land; the Buddhas of past, present, and future numerous as grains of sand in the Ganges River are Buddhas in one's own Pure Land.

Even Amitabha Buddha of the world of Bliss is simply one Buddha of one realm of one's own Pure Land.

Wei-tse

The Sword of Zen

Of old it has been said, "There are basically no words for the way, but we use words to illustrate the way." It is also said, "If speech does not avoid cliché, how can it get you out of bondage?"

If powerful people are like long swords against the sky, cold and stern, inviolable, then they will finally have some freedom.

The expedients of Zen masters are like bonfires: get close to them, and you lose your life. If you understand by thinking and know by pondering, you're a thousand miles away.

Wu-chien

The Great Way

The Great Way is always present, but though it's present, it's hard to see. If you want to understand the true essence of the way, do not get rid of sound and form, words and speech; words and speech are themselves the Great Way.

You do not need to remove afflictions; afflictions are originally empty and null. Arbitrary feelings may wrap you up, but all are like shadows, like echoes; who knows what is bad, what good?

If you consciously grasp forms as real, your insight into essence will surely be imperfect. If you deliberately perform works seeking Buddhahood, these works are major evidences of birth and death.

While works of birth and death always follow you, you remain unawakened in a pitch dark hell. Once you have realized the principle, there has never been a difference; after awakening, who is late, who early?

The realm of reality is as vast as cosmic space; it is the knowing mind of sentient beings that is small. Just as long as you do not become egotistic and selfish, you will be ever sated with the spiritual food of nirvana.

Pao-chih

The Straight Path

I announce the straight path to all people: nonbeing is in fact not nonexistence. Nonbeing and non-nonexistence are not two; why should we talk about voidness in contrast to being? Being and nonexistence are names set up by confused minds; when one is refuted, the other does not remain.

Both names are made by your feelings; when there are no feelings, there is basic reality as such. If you want to seek Buddha but keep your feelings, you are hauling a net up a mountain to snare fish: it is a useless waste of effort, without benefit. How long will you misuse your time?

If you do not understand that mind itself is Buddha, you are as if riding a donkey in search of a donkey. If you do not hate or love anything, this affliction should disappear.

To get rid of this, you must detach from

the body; when detached from the body, there is no Buddha, no cause. When no Buddha or cause can be grasped, there is naturally no doctrine or person.

Pao-chih

The Ingredients

It is laughable how slovenly people are, each holding onto a different view. They just want to stand by the pan, expecting a pancake; they do not know how to go back to the root and see the flour. The flour is the root of right and wrong; it changes in a hundred ways, depending on how people prepare it.

What is needed is to free the intellect in all ways, not to become partial or obsessed. Freedom from attachment is itself liberation; if you seek anything, you will again meet a snare. With a loving heart, be evenhanded to all, and the enlightenment of reality as such will spontaneously appear; if you keep a dualistic consciousness of others and self, you will not see the face of Buddha right in front of you.

Pao-chih

The Nonduality of Matter and Emptiness

The nature of things fundamentally has no color, but people idly create adornments. If you interpret cessation and contemplation through your ego, your own mind is in turmoil, unbalanced, mad.

If you do not know the subtle principle of complete penetration, when will you attain understanding of real eternity?

If you cannot cure your own sickness, and yet teach medicinal prescriptions to others, outwardly this may seem to be good, but inwardly you are like a rapacious beast.

The ignorant fear hell, but the wise consider it no different from heaven. If the mind is never aroused toward objects, then wherever you walk is the site of enlightenment.

Buddhas are not separate from people, but people create disparity themselves. If you want to get rid of the three poisons, you will never leave the conflagration; the wise know that mind is Buddha, while the ignorant wish for paradise.

Pao-chih

Naturalness

What is coming from nowhere? It means not depending on any practices.

What is going nowhere? It means not grasping any doctrine.

What is detachment from past existence? It means not dwelling on traces of the past, detaching from labels, and not intellectualizing anything.

What is detachment from present existence? It means the present mind is unaffected by the duality of being and nonbeing.

What is detachment from future existence? It means the mind does not grasp the future, but realizes the naturalness of things.

Fu Shan-hui

Virtue and Knowledge

As long as you are bound by all sorts of things, existent and nonexistent, you cannot be free. This is because you first possess virtue and knowledge before being firmly established in inner truth, so you are ridden by virtue and knowledge. It is like menials employing a noble.

It is better to settle the inner truth first, and then afterwards gain virtue and knowledge. Then if you need virtue and knowledge, as the occasion appears you will be able to turn gold into earth and earth into gold, change sea water into buttermilk, smash the polar mountain into dust, and place the waters of the four oceans into a single pore. You create unlimited meanings within one meaning, and make one meaning of unlimited meanings.

Pai-chang

Knowing and Being

There are people in the world who constantly lecture on scriptures and ethics, who know what is wrong and what is not wrong, what is sinful and what is not sinful, what is offensive and what is not offensive. They are outwardly proper in their bearing, but have not stopped bad patterns in their inner minds; are they able to attain liberation from miseries?

Suppose someone inwardly has full knowledge of cause and effect, and the various conditions for misery and happiness, and he is also proper and mannerly in outward appearance, yet cannot take care of himself, and keeps five hundred iron barbs inside his clothes—do you think this person can be free of pain? If people who study the way now are outwardly proper but inwardly do not stop bad patterns in their minds, they will be like this.

Fu Shan-hui

Insight

It has been asked, "The principle and knowledge of the subtle truth of suchness is mysterious and profound: how can those of shallow perceptions gain insight?"

One should not misrepresent Buddha—Buddha did not speak in this way. All things are neither deep nor shallow in themselves—it is just that you yourself don't see, and think that means extreme profundity.

When you have insight, everything you see is subtle; why put the bodhisattvas on a pedestal, or particularly set up sages? As Master Sheng said, 'It's not that knowledge is deep—things are deeper than knowledge.' This is just an expression of lament that knowledge cannot reach things.

Don't be discriminatory, don't keep a grasping and rejecting attitude. For this reason it is said, "Truth has no comparison, because it is not relative to anything."

The scriptures have body and mind for their meanings: the *Flower Ornament Scripture* says, "The body is the treasury of truths, the mind is the unobstructed lamp. Illuminating the emptiness of all things is called liberating people."

Hui-chung

Images and Relics

If you think you can become enlightened just by worshipping images and relics, this is a mistaken view. This is actually possession by the poisonous serpent of temptation.

Dogen

Discipline

If you insist upon disciplinary regulations and vegetarianism as fundamental, make them established practices, and think you can attain enlightenment that way, you are wrong.

Dogen

Overcoming Greed

If you would be free of greed, first you have to leave egotism behind. The best mental exercise for relinquishing egotism is contemplating impermanence.

Dogen

Tact

When you see others' errors and you want to
guide them because you think they are wrong
and you feel compassion for them, you
should employ tact to avoid angering them,
and contrive to appear as if you were talking
about something else.

Dogen

Emotional Views

Students of recent times cling to their own emotional views and go by their own subjective opinions, thinking Buddhism must be as they think it is, and denying it could be any different. As long as they are wandering in illusion seeking something resembling their own emotional judgments, most of them will make no progress on the way of enlightenment.

Dogen

Appearance and Reality

- Most people of the world want others to know when they have done something good, and want others not to know when they have done something bad.
- If you refrain from doing something because people would think ill of it, or if you try to do good so others will look upon you as a true Buddhist, these are still worldly feelings.
- If you have compassion and are imbued with the spirit of the Way, it is of no consequence to be criticized, even reviled, by the ignorant. But if you lack the spirit of the Way, you should be wary of being thought of by others as having the Way.
- What you think in your own mind to be good, or what people of the world think is good, is not necessarily good.
- If people who keep up appearances and

are attached to themselves gather together to study, not one of them will emerge with an awakened mind.

- You should not be esteemed by others if you have no real inner virtue. People here in Japan esteem others on the basis of outward appearances, without knowing anything about real inner virtue; so students lacking the spirit of the Way are dragged down into bad habits and become subject to temptation.

Dogen

Practicing Truth

- If you study a lot because you are worried that others will think badly of you for being ignorant and you'll feel stupid, this is a serious mistake.
- People of the world cannot necessarily be considered good—let them think whatever they will.
- To "leave the world" means that you do not let the feelings of worldly people hang on your mind.
- You should not do what is bad just because no one will see it or know of it.
- You should think about the fact that you will surely die. This truth is indisputable.
- Even if you don't think about the inevitability of death, you should determine not to pass your time in vain.
- Our lives are only here for now.

- One should not differentiate good and bad on the basis of taste.
- One need not necessarily depend on the words of the ancients, but must only think of what is really true.
- If you want to travel the Way of Buddhas and Zen masters, then expect nothing, seek nothing, and grasp nothing.

Dogen

Morals

- The ancients thought it shameful to seek advancement or to want to be the head of something, or the chief or senior.
- No one should torment people or break their hearts.
- Just regard people's virtues, don't be obsessed with their faults.
- People should cultivate secret virtue.
- No matter how bad a state of mind you may get into, if you keep strong and hold out, eventually the floating clouds must vanish and the withering wind must cease.
- Do not be so proud as to hope to equal the great sages; do not be so mean as to hope to equal the ignoble.
- If one pursued selfish schemes to stay alive, there would be no end to it.
- There is fundamentally no good or bad

in the human mind; good and bad arise according to circumstances.

- Though a nobleman's power is greater than that of an ox, he does not contend with an ox.
- To plow deep but plant shallow is a way to natural disaster; if you help yourself but harm others, how could there be no consequences?

Dogen

the pocket zen reader

Understanding

- Don't cling to your own understanding. Even if you do understand something, you should ask yourself if there might be something you have not fully resolved, or if there may be some higher meaning yet.
- Although a suspicious mind is bad, still it is wrong to cling to what you shouldn't believe in, or to fail to ask about a truth you should seek.
- Even if you have thoroughly studied the stories of the ancients and you sit constantly like iron or stone, as long as you are attached to yourself you cannot find the Way of the enlightened, ever.
- Although the Way is complete in everyone, realization of the Way depends on a combination of conditions.
- Tenacious opinionation is not transmit-

ted by your parents; it is just that you have tacitly come to believe in opinions for no reason other than that over time you have picked up what people say.

- Whether or not beginners are imbued with the spirit of the Way, they should carefully read and study the sagacious teachings of the scriptures and treatises.
- Once having understood, you should read the teachings of the sages many times.
- Truth is not greater or lesser, but people are shallow or deep.

Dogen

Attitude

- Even if you are in a high place, don't forget you may fall. Even if you are safe, don't forget danger. Even though you are alive today, don't assume you will be alive tomorrow.
- The mind has no fixed characteristics; depending on circumstances, it may turn out any way at all.
- Even if it is painful and lonely, associate with worthy companions.
- Consider how you will travel the path, without taking notice of slander from others, without heeding resentment from others.
- Do not think of studying Buddhism in order to gain some advantage as a reward for practicing Buddhism.
- Everyone has great faults, and pride is the greatest fault.

- Prefer to be defeated in the presence of the wise than to excel among fools.
- If the mentality that seeks honor and advantage does not cease, you will be ill at ease all your life.
- Students of the Way must individually examine their own selves. To examine yourself means to reflect upon how you should carry yourself, mentally and physically.
- If the heart is not empty, it will not admit truthful words.

Dogen

Presence

- If you don't understand the Way as it meets your eyes, how can you know the Path as you walk?
- Progress is not a matter of far or near.
- All things have their function; it is a matter of use in the appropriate situation.
- Don't waste time.

Shih-t'ou

Cultism

How could it be permissible to form a cult,
gather followers and cronies, dash off writings, and toil in pursuit of objects for love of
honor and advantage?

Tung-shan

Clarity

- If you can forget both clamor and silence, you will surely understand the simultaneous realization of the absolute and the relative.
- Buy afterwards; try first.
- All obstructions due to actions come from false conceptions.
- Only a clear mind knows itself.

Lin-ch'uan

Waking Up

- The body of Buddha fills the cosmos, manifest to all sentient beings everywhere.
- The peak experience lights up the heavens and covers the earth, illumines past and present.
- The great cause of the Buddhas is not apart from your daily affairs.
- Look with intense concentration at the state before any forms are distinguished, before any illustration is evident.
- The sphere of perfect communion is clear everywhere—why are people in such a hurry?

Daio

Mind Matters

If you misunderstand your mind, you are an ordinary mortal; if you understand your mind, you are a sage.

In this it makes no difference whether you are a male or female, old or young, smart or simple.

Jakushitsu

Zen in Action

If you wish to understand yourself, you must succeed in doing so in the midst of all kinds of confusions and upsets. Don't make the mistake of sitting dead in the cold ashes of a withered tree.

Emyo

Getting it Right

- What is the benefit of exerting mental effort in the wrong way?
- Realization without making sure of right and wrong is of dubious benefit.

Guon

Realization

- Zen is not a conception—if you set up an idea of it, you turn away from the source.
- The Way is beyond cultivated effects; if you set up accomplishment, you lose the essence.
- After having killed all, you see that mountains are mountains, rivers are rivers.
- Let go over a mile-high precipice, and appear with your whole body throughout the universe.
- Sitting peacefully on a cushion day and night seeking to attain Buddhahood, rejecting life and death in hopes of realizing enlightenment, is all like a monkey grasping at the moon reflected in the water.
- See for yourself.

- Plunge boldly into the Beyond, then be free wherever you are.
- Letting go of all objects and letting all things rest is the foremost technique, but if you stick to this technique it is not right.
- Those with higher knowledge and keen faculties penetrate through to great realization without needing explanations, devices, or objectives.

Shoitsu

Everyday Zen

- People see others in terms of themselves. If you are ambitious, that is the way you see others. If you are greedy, you see others in terms of desire.
- It is easy to keep things at a distance. It is harder to be aloof of them.
- When you are deluded, you are used by your body. When you are enlightened, you use your body.
- If there is any judgment in your heart, it will be blocked by the judgment.
- There is no Buddha outside your heart. Always keep a pure, clean heart.
- It is only necessary to see and hear directly.
- If you actually manage to see your basic mind, you must treat it as if you were raising an infant.

Bunan

Observations

- The poor suffer from want, the rich suffer from possessions. The upper classes suffer from their high status, the lower classes suffer from their low status.
- When you die, you go alone. Who goes with you? What can you take along with you?
- Although their fundamental essence is the same, awakened people turn inward while emotional and intellectual people pursue externals.
- If you want to realize the essence that is the same as all Buddhas, first you must clearly understand the root of ignorance.
- When people seeking enlightenment see forms, they question what it is that sees. When they hear, they question what it is that hears. When they feel, they question what it is that feels. When they

know something, they question what it is that knows.

- When you walk, practice while walking. When you rest, practice while resting. When you speak, practice while speaking.
- When you're busy and easily distracted, question what it is that gets distracted.
- In a single day an ordinary person "transmigrates" countless times, rarely keeping a human mind, much less roam in heavenly states.

Torei

Zen Proverbs

- What is appropriate provisionally does not suit the real.
- Unless the medicine stuns you, it won't cure the disease.
- If you want both eyes to be perfectly clear, you must not dwell on mental or physical elements, and not get entangled in objects.
- Flowing water doesn't go stale.
- Whoever receives a salary without doing any service is uneasy sleeping and eating.
- Not being present, even temporarily, is like being dead.
- Who can be master in any place and meet the source in everything?
- You too can be host within the world, and also come as a guest from outside creation.
- It is not gotten from another.

- A petty officer often thinks of the rules; a seasoned general doesn't talk of soldiering.
- The hungry will eat anything; the thirsty will drink anything.
- Government officials are easily tested, but that doesn't finish the matter.
- Not falling into causality is forced denial; not being blind to causality is finding the wondrous along with the flow.
- Just do good; don't ask about the road ahead.
- Strictly executing the absolute imperative is still but half the issue.
- When your heart is crooked, you don't realize your tongue is forked.
- If you have a reason, you don't need to shout.
- Outwardly, do not react; inwardly, do not dwell in emptiness. Outwardly, do not pursue ramifications; inwardly, do not remain in trance.
- Sweeping away tracks makes traces, all

the more evident the more you try to
hide.

- Suspicion in the mind makes ghosts in
  the dark.
- Are there any elephant tusks in a rat's
  mouth?
- The nobility of the ancients was no more
  than purity and serenity—what need for
  bushels of emblems?
- Don't brag so much.
- When the house is rich, the children are
  haughty.
- Overindulging people is folly.

Library of Congress
Cataloging-in-Publication Data

The pocket Zen reader/compiled and
translated by Thomas Cleary.
—1st ed.
p.   cm.
ISBN 1-57062-447-X (paper: alk. paper)
1. Zen Buddhism—Quotation, maxism, etc.
I. Cleary, Thomas F., 1949–   .
BQ9267.P63   1999   98-39908
294.3′927—dc21   CIP

(Continued on next page)

THE TIBETAN BOOK OF THE DEAD
Translated by Francesca Fremantle and
Chögyam Trungpa

WALDEN by Henry David Thoreau

THE WAY OF MYTH:
Talking with Joseph Campbell
by Fraser Boa

WAYS OF THE CHRISTIAN MYSTICS
by Thomas Merton

WRITING DOWN THE BONES by Natalie Goldberg

ZEN ESSENCE: THE SCIENCE OF FREEDOM
Translated and edited by Thomas Cleary

ZEN FLESH, ZEN BONES:
A Collection of Zen and Pre-Zen Writings
Compiled by Paul Reps & Nyogen Senzaki

ZEN LESSONS: THE ART OF LEADERSHIP
Translated by Thomas Cleary

For a complete list, send for our catalogue:

Shambhala Publications
P.O. Box 308
Boston, MA 02117–0308